Especially For

MY SON - C BAS

From

DAD

Date

JUNE 8TH, 2015

JOANNA
BLOSS

CLASS
OF
2015

Bible Memory Plan & Devotional
for **Graduates**

A Hope and a Future
Jeremiah 29:11

BARBOUR BOOKS
An Imprint of Barbour Publishing, Inc.

Scripture quotations marked NIV are taken from the HOLY BIBLE, NEW INTERNATIONAL VERSION®. NIV®. Copyright © 1973, 1978, 1984, 2011 by Biblica, Inc.™ Used by permission. All rights reserved worldwide.

Scripture quotations marked NLT are taken from the Holy Bible, New Living Translation copyright© 1996, 2004, 2007 by Tyndale House Foundation. Used by permission of Tyndale House Publishers, Inc. Carol Stream, Illinois 60188. All rights reserved.

Scripture quotations marked CEV are from the Contemporary English Version, Copyright © 1995 by American Bible Society. Used by permission.

Published by Barbour Books, an imprint of Barbour Publishing, Inc., P.O. Box 719, Uhrichsville, Ohio 44683, www.barbourbooks.com

Our mission is to publish and distribute inspirational products offering exceptional value and biblical encouragement to the masses.

Member of the
Evangelical Christian
Publishers Association

Printed in the United States of America.

Contents

Endings and Beginnings

Congratulations! As this chapter of your life comes to an end, you no doubt have some mixed feelings. Endings can be sad; saying good-bye is hard. But the sadness is bittersweet. After all, new chapters hold so much promise! Your bright future brings new experiences, friends, and countless opportunities to depend on God. Despite the big dreams you have for this next season of life, remember that transitions can be hard. Reality won't always match your expectations. Things might be harder than you first imagined them. But hang in there. You'll eventually master the learning curve, and in no time at all you'll settle into a new life, a new routine, and a new awareness of God's presence in your soul.

Life is often compared to a journey. There are hills and valleys, the terrain is sometimes rough, and other times the path is level. The weather can change frequently—storm clouds roll in and suddenly disappear. Just like any journey, its success depends on how well you've prepared. God's Word is the most important provision you will ever need for this journey called life. The Bible speaks to every circumstance we could possibly face. Sure, you can carry it with you, but if you commit His Word to memory, you'll never be caught without it. The pages that follow contain devotionals with relevant verses for you to memorize, as well as a plan for how to keep it fresh in your mind as you start on the journey of life.

God Loves You

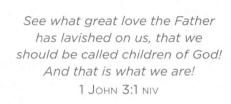

*See what great love the Father
has lavished on us, that we
should be called children of God!
And that is what we are!*

1 John 3:1 NIV

Karl Barth was a famous teacher and theologian. He was a great thinker who explained deep, spiritual truths so others could understand. Someone once asked Barth to share what he thought was the most profound spiritual truth. They no doubt waited expectantly for this intellectual to expound upon a complicated theological concept. Instead, Barth said, "Jesus loves me! This I know, for the Bible tells me so."

God's truth is that simple. It changes *everything*, and yet we understand so little of His love! In our efforts to be profound, we often miss the simplicity of the deep connection God longs to have with us. As the old hymn says, "the love of God, is greater far, than tongue or pen can ever tell." Pray that God would begin to expand your understanding of His great and mighty love for you.

Jesus loves me! This I know,
For the Bible tells me so;
Little ones to Him belong;
They are weak, but He is strong.
Yes, Jesus loves me!
Yes, Jesus loves me!
Yes, Jesus loves me!
The Bible tells me so.

This song was originally a poem written by Anna B. Warner. Over the years it has become one of the most beloved children's songs of all time.

No matter who we are, these simple words touch a chord in our hearts. What an amazing feeling it is to be loved!

These verses talk about the deep, deep love of God. As you commit them to memory, pray that God will help you understand more fully what His love means to you.

*Long ago the L*ORD *said to Israel:*
"I have loved you, my people,
with an everlasting love. With unfailing
love I have drawn you to myself."
JEREMIAH 31:3 NLT

◆

God loved the people of this world so
much that he gave his only Son, so that
everyone who has faith in him will have
eternal life and never really die.
JOHN 3:16 CEV

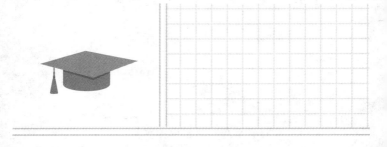

And may you have the power to understand,
as all God's people should, how wide, how long,
how high, and how deep his love is. May you
experience the love of Christ, though it is too
great to understand fully. Then you will be
made complete with all the fullness of life
and power that comes from God.

Ephesians 3:18–19 NLT

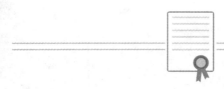

The Deadly Catch

Sin pays off with death.
But God's gift is eternal life given
by Jesus Christ our Lord.
ROMANS 6:23 CEV

If it sounds too good to be true, it probably is. No matter how good the offer, there's almost always a catch. They call it the fine print, because it's easy to miss. This is especially true with sin. In the Garden of Eden, Adam and Eve were lured by Satan's sales pitch. They were blinded by the delectable fruit and made the terrible mistake of ignoring the fine print. The Bible is clear about the cost of sin: "[It] pays off with death." No matter how fun or alluring it may appear, there's *always* a catch. A deadly catch.

That's the bad news. The Good News is that you have been given a gift—it's certainly not free— it cost God's Son His life. But it is bought and paid for, and it is yours for the taking.

Have you trusted Christ as your Savior? The Romans Road is a series of verses found in the book of Romans that explain the plan of salvation in a simple and clear way. Here are some of the verses:

- ▶ All are sinners (Romans 3:23; Romans 3:10)
- ▶ Sin brings death (Romans 5:12)
- ▶ God loves us; Christ died for our sins (Romans 5:8)
- ▶ Christ's death brings eternal life (Romans 6:23)
- ▶ Say it out loud and believe in your heart that Jesus is Lord—eternal life is the gift! (Romans 10:9-10)

If you have not yet taken hold of God's promise for you, now would be the perfect time! As you prayerfully meditate on the following verses, commit them to memory. You might even copy them on index cards to carry with you. Now you are equipped to share the Good News with others!

*For all have sinned and fall
short of the glory of God.*
Romans 3:23 NIV

—————— ◈ ——————

*But God showed his great love for
us by sending Christ to die for us
while we were still sinners.*
Romans 5:8 NLT

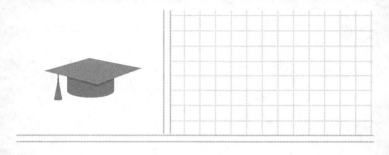

*If you openly declare that Jesus is
Lord and believe in your heart that God
raised him from the dead, you will be saved.
For it is by believing in your heart that you
are made right with God, and it is by openly
declaring your faith that you are saved.*

ROMANS 10:9–10 NLT

God's Plans

For we are God's masterpiece.
He has created us anew in Christ
Jesus, so we can do the good things
he planned for us long ago.

EPHESIANS 2:10 NLT

Masterpiece: The word itself is pretty descriptive, but how often do we really think about what it means? A masterpiece is an artist's best piece of work, a showpiece. The masterpiece stops everyone in their tracks and causes them to truly appreciate the work of the creator.

The Bible says *you* are God's masterpiece! You are His greatest piece of work. It's hard to believe sometimes, but His Word is true. Long ago, God made plans for you, plans that you've only begun to dream of.

The specifics vary for each of us, but our purpose is all the same. God created us to do *good things*.

What good things does God have planned for you today?

Young adults are often told they should find themselves. However, this search can take people far from where they're meant to be. Many people justify poor decisions and destructive living patterns with the excuse that they were only trying to "find themselves."

But knowing ourselves is only helpful to the degree that we also know *whose* we are. Understanding who we are in Christ radically transforms our lives. It enables us to make decisions that are less selfish and more God centered. The more we get to know the truth about ourselves—from God's point of view—the more freedom we have to live as His masterpieces.

If you are a child of God, then these scriptures tell the truth about you.

You are:

▸ Chosen, holy, and beloved (Colossians 3:12)

▸ Made complete in Christ (Colossians 2:10)

▸ No longer in darkness (John 8:12)

▸ Redeemed and forgiven (Ephesians 1:7)

▸ Set free (Galatians 5:1)

*God is the one who began this good
work in you, and I am certain that he
won't stop before it is complete on
the day that Christ Jesus returns.*

PHILIPPIANS 1:6 CEV

*And we know that God causes
everything to work together for the
good of those who love God and are
called according to his purpose for them.*

ROMANS 8:28 NLT

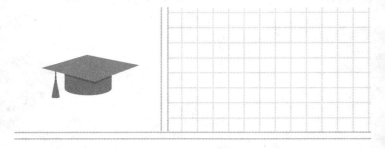

"My thoughts are nothing like your thoughts,"
says the LORD. "And my ways are far beyond
anything you could imagine."

ISAIAH 55:8 NLT

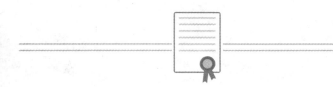

Staying on the Path

You have accepted Christ Jesus as your Lord. Now keep on following him. Plant your roots in Christ and let him be the foundation for your life. Be strong in your faith, just as you were taught. And be grateful.

COLOSSIANS 2:6–7 CEV

It's an awful feeling to be lost. Wrong turns lead to unfamiliar surroundings, which lead to feelings of fear and anxiety.

From time to time, we all feel lost in life. We can be unsure of our way and feel as if we are wandering in circles. But the Bible offers good advice for staying on course. We need to:

▸ Follow Christ

▸ Plant ourselves in Him

▸ Allow Him be the foundation of our lives

▸ Grow in our faith

▸ Be thankful

Though it's hard to do all these things consistently, it's worth the effort to stay on the path He has for us.

21

Being an adult can be such a pain. There are so many decisions to make! Go to college? Which one? Declare a major? What if I don't like it? Get a job? Date? Travel? So many decisions, so many opportunities to take a wrong turn! The thought of making decisions about the rest of our lives can be paralyzing. It's enough to make us want to live like Peter Pan—just refuse to grow up. Wouldn't it be nice if we could do an Internet search for directions? Just type in "what should I do next?" and wait for the step-by-step guide to appear.

The Bible provides this for us. God consistently promises to lead us in the direction He wants us to go. Discerning God's will for our lives can feel like walking blindly, in the dark, but memorizing scripture can light the way. Commit to memorizing the following verses over the next week or so, and ask God to reveal where He wants you to go:

You are my God. Show me what you want me to do, and let your gentle Spirit lead me in the right path.
PSALM 143:10 CEV

The Lord gives me strength. He makes my feet as sure as those of a deer, and he helps me stand on the mountains.
HABAKKUK 3:19 CEV

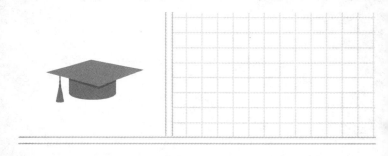

*Do what the Lord wants, and he will give
you your heart's desire. Let the Lord
lead you and trust him to help.*

PSALM 37:4-5 CEV

Confident Faith

*Faith is the confidence that what
we hope for will actually happen;
it gives us assurance about
things we cannot see.*

HEBREWS 11:1 NLT

If you have flown in an airplane, you have exercised faith. You probably have no idea how a 175,000 pound jet plane can lift itself into the sky—and stay there—for hours on end. However, if you want to fly, you have no choice but to trust in the designer and builder of the aircraft, the mechanics, and the pilots in charge. This faith isn't blind. It is grounded in the reputation of the airline, government regulations, and physics itself.

Faith in God is not blind either. You have every good reason to trust Him. His Word tells you everything you need to know about Him, so you can confidently rest in His truth and promises. Let that faith take you to where He wants you to go.

A mustard seed is barely the size of a pinhead, but under the right conditions can grow into an enormous tree. When the disciples lamented their lack of faith, Jesus encouraged them with the picture of a mustard seed. "You just need a little," He said. "God's power does the work!"

Growing your faith is similar to growing a mustard tree. You start with a tiny seed, planted in a small cup of dirt. You gently water it, keep it in the light, expectantly watching for signs of growth. When it finally sprouts, you transplant it to roomy, fertile ground. You continue to water and care for it, day after day.

Our faith grows in much the same way. Prayer, reading God's Word, fellowshipping with other Christians, and exercising dependence on Him are all ways we can cultivate a rich life of faith.

Be diligent. The harvest is worth the wait!

So faith comes from hearing, that is,
hearing the Good News about Christ.
ROMANS 10:17 NLT

The apostles said to the Lord,
"Increase our faith!"
LUKE 17:5 NIV

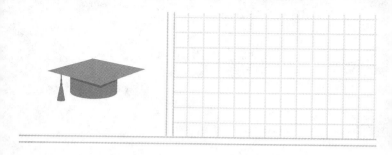

*And without faith it is impossible to please God,
because anyone who comes to him must
believe that he exists and that he rewards
those who earnestly seek him.*

HEBREWS 11:6 NIV

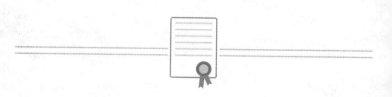

First Things First

*But more than anything else,
put God's work first and do what
he wants. Then the other things
will be yours as well.*
MATTHEW 6:33 CEV

Imagine an empty jar. Next to the jar are large
rocks, sand, pebbles, and water. The challenge is to
make room in the jar for all those things. The order
is important. Starting with water or sand means
the other items won't fit. Beginning with the large
rocks allows the pebbles, sand, and water to fill in
the gaps.

And so it is with priorities. It is easy to get
caught up in the sand and pebbles of life: watching
TV, staying up too late and sleeping even later,
spending money on too many extras like soft
drinks and candy.

The older we get the more choices we have.
But if we put all those unimportant things first,
there won't be room for the things that matter.
God's Word says to put His work first. When we
do that, everything else will nicely fall into place.

As a young adult, you will likely have more discretionary time than at any other time in your life. Even if you have work and school obligations, if you don't have a family to care for or a home to maintain, you will have many options for how to spend your time. In our plugged-in, instant world, there are also plenty of ways to procrastinate. Have you ever found yourself running out of time for the things you really need to accomplish? Time management experts suggest doing the most important things first. Regardless of how you choose to spend your time, make a commitment to put God's Word first in your life.

Write the following verses on sticky notes or make screen shots of them for the background on your phone. Take the first five minutes of every day to focus on these words, and rehearse them as you drive to work or school.

But blessed is the one who trusts in the LORD, whose confidence is in him.
JEREMIAH 17:7 NIV

For physical training is of some value, but godliness has value for all things, holding promise for both the present life and the life to come.
1 TIMOTHY 4:8 NIV

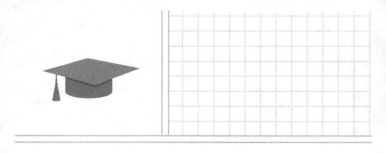

You cannot be the slave of two masters.
You will like one more than the other
or be more loyal to one than to the other.
You cannot serve God and money.

LUKE 16:13 CEV

The Greatest Book

All Scripture is inspired by God and is useful to teach us what is true and to make us realize what is wrong in our lives. It corrects us when we are wrong and teaches us to do what is right.

2 TIMOTHY 3:16 NLT

Easily the best-selling book of all time, the Bible is a God-inspired wonder. From Genesis to Revelation, consistent themes are woven throughout its pages. God's love for us, the problem of sin, and His plan to save us are told over and over again by over forty authors whose lives spanned over fifteen hundred years. There are over twenty-five hundred prophecies in the Bible, and scholars tell us that today at least two thousand of these are already fulfilled.

God's Word is truth, inspired by Him across generations. As relevant to us as they were a thousand years ago, the themes in scripture connect humankind with ancient truths about our Creator, our Savior, and our Comforter.

No matter where life takes you, you can be sure that God's Word is useful, helpful, accurate, and relevant for every situation you could possibly encounter.

Long before there were printing presses or computers or e-mail, human beings depended on oral tradition to pass along information. Stories were passed down from generation to generation and treasured in the hearts of the listeners and tellers. Often, stories were put to poems or music. These people knew then what neuroscientists tell us now—that putting words to music can greatly enhance our ability to recall them. The rhythm, alliteration, rhyme, and structure of music can help us recall songs we learned years ago as little children. (Some of us probably still have to sing the alphabet to keep the letters in order!)

Putting the words of Scripture to song is a simple and effective way to memorize God's Word. Regardless of how musical you are, see if you can come up with a few simple tunes to help you memorize the following verses:

*I have hidden your word in my heart
that I might not sin against you.*
Psalm 119:11 niv

---

*Heaven and earth will disappear,
but my words will never disappear.*
Matthew 24:35 nlt

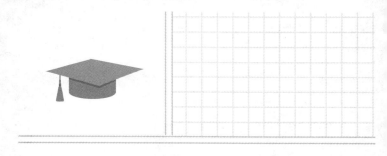

*Our Lord, you bless everyone who lives right
and obeys your Law. You bless all of those who
follow your commands from deep in their hearts
and who never do wrong or turn from you.*

PSALM 119:1–3 CEV

Free to Serve

My friends, you were chosen to be free. So don't use your freedom as an excuse to do anything you want. Use it as an opportunity to serve each other with love.

GALATIANS 5:13 CEV

When we are young, we long to be older. We dream about the day when we will be free. Free to stay up as late as we want, to eat junk food for dinner, to come and go as we please. The prospect of the freedom that comes with adulthood can be so enticing.

However, every adult knows it's not all fun and games. Eleanor Roosevelt once said, "Freedom makes a huge requirement of every human being. With freedom comes responsibility. For the person who is unwilling to grow up, the person who does not want to carry his own weight, this is a frightening prospect."

In Galatians, Paul reminds us of the responsibility that comes with freedom. One of the most God-honoring ways to use our freedom is to serve one another. How can you serve others today?

We are surrounded by opportunities to serve others, but we sometimes miss them. It is important to prepare, because the moments often come up unexpectedly. Here are some ideas to make serving others fit more naturally into your day:

- ▶ Begin in prayer. Ask God to open your eyes to those in need.
- ▶ Keep a few "survival kits" in your car to give away. Include things like bottled water, grocery store gift cards, lip balm, hand lotion, tissues, toothbrush, and toothpaste.
- ▶ Volunteer! If we all just gave one hour a week, imagine the difference it would make.
- ▶ Say thank you.
- ▶ Buy coffee for the person behind you in line.
- ▶ Offer to bring a meal to someone who is homebound.

Above all, ask the Lord to give you a servant's heart and use your gifts and abilities to do good for others. The more you serve, the more you'll see!

*If you are wise and understand God's ways,
prove it by living an honorable life, doing good
works with the humility that comes from wisdom.*
JAMES 3:13 NLT

*Each of you should use whatever gift you have
received to serve others, as faithful stewards of
God's grace in its various forms.*
1 PETER 4:10 NIV

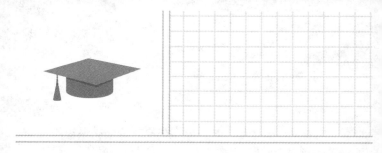

*If you want to be great, you must be the servant
of all the others. And if you want to be first,
you must be the slave of the rest.*

MATTHEW 20:26–27 CEV

Our Desires

*Those who belong to Christ Jesus
have nailed the passions and desires
of their sinful nature to his cross and
crucified them there.*

GALATIANS 5:24 NLT

"What is it that you want?" Can you imagine God asking you this question?

Think of Solomon, the young king. One night God came to him in a dream and said, "Solomon, ask for anything you want, and I will give it to you" (1 Kings 3:5 CEV). Many young men of that day, and many of us today, would be tempted to ask for wealth or power or long life. But Solomon had a different perspective. He recognized that these are temporary and ultimately sinful desires. Instead of a selfish pursuit, Solomon humbly asked for wisdom. God was pleased and granted the desire of his heart. God granted Solomon's request because Solomon's desires were in line with *His* desires.

God longs to give you the desires of your heart—ask Him to keep His desires at the center of your life.

Since ancient times, people have used fasting as a way to demonstrate their desire to grow closer to God. In Joel 2:12, God beckons His people to come to Him in repentance "with fasting and weeping and mourning" (NIV). In Psalms, David writes about his deep longing for God in the parched desert. Jesus spent forty days in the desert, without food or water, in preparation for His earthly ministry.

When we experience true physical hunger or thirst, we are reminded of our frailty and our utter dependence on Him. Our minds become acutely aware of our need. Fasting from food for a short time can be a way to cleanse ourselves and come back to God.

We can take "fasting" breaks from other things as well. We can fast from television or smart phones, computers, or even sugar, to help draw us closer to God, especially when we replace the time when we would normally be using these things with time for prayer and communication with Him.

Set aside a time each week to "fast" from something that you hold dear. Commit to using this time to meditate on and memorize God's Word, so that your desires will continue to be molded into His.

O God, you are my God; I earnestly search for you. My soul thirsts for you; my whole body longs for you in this parched and weary land where there is no water.

PSALM 63:1 NLT

May he grant your heart's desires and make all your plans succeed.

PSALM 20:4 NLT

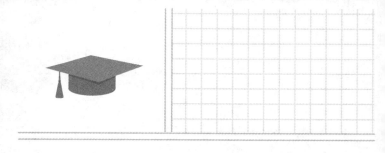

*You will seek me and find me when
you seek me with all your heart.*

JEREMIAH 29:13 NIV

God's Promises

I praise God for what he has
promised. I trust in God,
so why should I be afraid?
What can mere mortals do to me?

PSALM 56:4 NLT

The book of Psalms, perhaps more than any other book in the Bible, captures the depth and breadth of human emotion. The first chapter describes the contrast of good and evil people, using the metaphor of a tree growing by the river to paint a picture of what our Father longs to do in our lives. We read of loneliness, despair, indescribable joy, and, through it all, a silver lining of hope behind every cloud. With each rise and fall of the writers' feelings, woven through this incredible volume is the golden thread of God's precious promises. He will never leave us. He will never forsake us. He will ultimately bring good from evil and set the world right.

Throughout the ups and downs of your life, be sure to revisit the book of Psalms frequently—you will never cease to be reminded and amazed at God's promises.

Thousands of promises are contained in God's Word. In 1886, the composer Russell Carter was surely inspired by them as he penned the words to this familiar hymn:

Standing on the promises of Christ my King,
Through eternal ages let his praises ring;
Glory in the highest, I will shout and sing,
Standing on the promises of God.
Standing, standing,
Standing on the promises of God my Savior;
Standing, standing,
I'm standing on the promises of God.

When Carter was still a young man, he was told he had a serious heart condition and that there was nothing doctors could do for him. Perhaps more than at any other time in his life, he leaned heavily on God's promises, believing in the truth of His Word.

When we memorize scripture, it is important to let the words sink into the depths of our souls.

Before memorizing the following verses, take a moment to paraphrase them into your own words and reflect upon their meaning. How do these ancient and enduring promises impact your life today?

*God made great and marvelous promises,
so that his nature would become part of us.
Then we could escape our evil desires and the
corrupt influences of this world.*
2 PETER 1:4 CEV

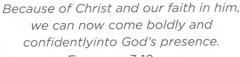

*Because of Christ and our faith in him,
we can now come boldly and
confidentlyinto God's presence.*
EPHESIANS 3:12 NLT

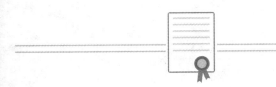

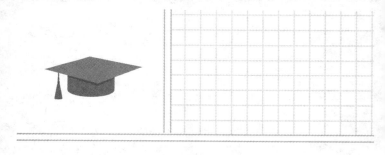

My sheep know my voice, and I know them.
They follow me, and I give them eternal life,
so that they will never be lost. No one can
snatch them out of my hand.

JOHN 10:27–28 CEV

Work Is Not a Bad Word

*Work willingly at whatever you do,
as though you were working for the
L*ORD* rather than for people.*

COLOSSIANS 3:23 NLT

"Friday's coming!" "It's finally the weekend!" "I hate Mondays!"

When did *work* get to be such a negative word? Many people consider their work drudgery, something only to be endured until clock-out time. They celebrate all weekend, then drag themselves back on Monday morning, only to perform the same endless cycle all over again.

In reality, God created us to work. Adam, the first man to work at the first job, was given the time-consuming but fascinating job of naming all the animals. As God brought each creature to him, Adam must have been completely amazed by His Father's creativity. When we work—willingly, and for the Lord—we can find incredible purpose and joy.

As you begin to discover your life's work, ask God to help you find work that you can be passionate about and do for Him.

Whether we stay home with small children or run a multimillion-dollar corporation, we will work in some form or fashion for our entire lives. There is tremendous value in work, and the Bible is clear about the need to work hard.

Hard work keeps us out of trouble, gives our minds focus, and protects us from depression and anxiety. It helps us contribute and keeps us from becoming entitled or taking others for granted. When we feel productive and busy, our minds are less likely to wander into dark places.

However, there are downsides to work. We can work for the wrong things, like power or money or success, while the Bible says we should ultimately work for eternal life. We can become consumed with our work, to the point that we ignore other people and responsibilities. Like most things in life, hard work requires a balanced mind.

Whether you commute to a job or school, copy these verses on the inside of your notebook or place them in a prominent position in your cubicle. Make a commitment to memorizing these three verses that outline God's position on work.

"Don't work for food that spoils. Work for food that gives eternal life. The Son of Man will give you this food, because God the Father has given him the right to do so."
JOHN 6:27 CEV

* * *

Try your best to live quietly, to mind your own business, and to work hard, just as we taught you to do.
1 THESSALONIANS 4:11 CEV

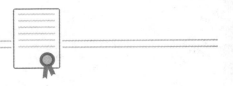

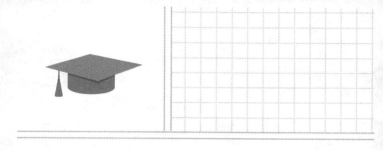

Don't fall in love with money. Be satisfied with
what you have. The Lord has promised that
he will not leave us or desert us.

HEBREWS 13:5 CEV

Eyes on Jesus

"There is only one thing worth being concerned about. Mary has discovered it, and it will not be taken away from her."

LUKE 10:42 NLT

Little sisters can be so annoying. Surely this is the way Martha felt when she was busy preparing for a visit from their dear friend Jesus. There was so much left to do to get dinner on the table. Martha couldn't believe how Mary could just calmly sit there and do nothing! Finally her frustration boiled over, and Martha burst into the room. "Tell her to help me, Lord!" Jesus must have felt bad for Martha, in her anxieties and worry. She was so consumed with unimportant details. "Come, sit with me." He beckoned. "Your sister Mary has chosen the most important thing. I long to share it with you."

What busyness and unimportant details are consuming your life today? Why not put them aside and spend some time at the feet of your Master?

Our goals reflect our desires. Without clear goals for our lives, we are prone to wander. Both large and small goals can shape the direction of our lives.

In the business world, we are often taught to think of SMART goals. The acronym reminds us to make goals that are specific, measureable, attainable, realistic, and timely. SMART goals can help us with education, career decisions, friendships, and fitness. Smart goals can also be a valuable tool to aid us in our spiritual lives. Take a look at how the following verses reflect SMART goals:

One thing I ask from the LORD, this only do I seek: that I may dwell in the house of the LORD all the days of my life, to gaze on the beauty of the LORD and to seek him in his temple.
PSALM 27:4 NIV

David's goal is quite specific: to dwell in God's house all of his days, to gaze on God's beauty, and to seek Him in His temple.

This verse reminds us that God gives us the strength to achieve our spiritual goals, which makes them realistic and attainable

*Look to the L*ORD *and his strength;*
seek his face always.
PSALM 105:4 NIV

The last thing a SMART goal suggests is giving it a time frame. Psalm 105:4 does this perfectly—all the days of our lives!

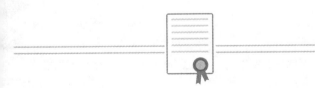

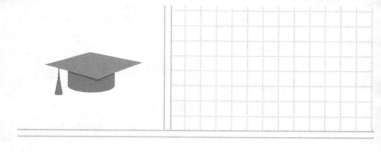

"The Lᴏʀᴅ bless you and keep you;
the Lᴏʀᴅ make his face shine on you and be
gracious to you; the Lᴏʀᴅ turn his face
toward you and give you peace."

Nᴜᴍʙᴇʀs 6:24-26 ɴɪᴠ

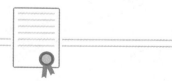

The Wise Book

The fear of the L<small>ORD</small> is the beginning of wisdom, and knowledge of the Holy One is understanding.

P<small>ROVERBS</small> 9:10 <small>NIV</small>

Mark Twain once said, "When I was ten, I thought my parents knew everything. When I became twenty, I was convinced they knew nothing. Then, at thirty, I realized I was right when I was ten."

Over the years, many books have been compiled of letters that parents have written to their children. They contain timeless wisdom, applicable to so many areas of our lives. Like Mark Twain, it is often not until we are older that we begin to appreciate the wisdom our parents have to offer. The book of Proverbs contains a wealth of wisdom passed down from Solomon to his son. From friendships, to managing money, to marriage and work, there is wisdom in Proverbs for every situation life brings our way.

Throughout your life, make it a habit to return to the book of Proverbs again and again. There you will always find an invaluable nugget of wisdom.

Use the acronym "WISE" to remind you of this important concept:

W-Well-informed. Colossians says, "Let the message about Christ completely fill your lives." Reading God's Word regularly and meditating on what it says increases our knowledge.

I-Insightful. Knowledge is good, but it is not enough. James 1:23-24 says, "If you hear the message and don't obey it, you are like people who stare at themselves in a mirror and forget what they look like as soon as they leave" (CEV). We must apply knowledge if we are to be wise.

S-Sound. Proverbs 4:7 reminds us to "develop good judgment" (NLT). Another way to say it? Be of sound mind. Wisdom not only *applies* the knowledge, but it knows *when* and *how* to do so.

E-Experienced. The more we experience God's teachings and apply them to our lives, the less likely we are to forget them. Then, as Colossians says, we can use that wisdom gained from experience to teach and instruct others.

Get wisdom. It's the wisest thing you can do.

I won't ever forget your teachings, because you give me new life by following them.
PSALM 119:93 CEV

———◆———

Getting wisdom is the wisest thing you can do! And whatever else you do, develop good judgment.
PROVERBS 4:7 NLT

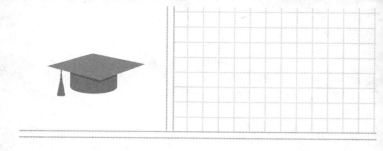

Let the message about Christ completely fill your
lives, while you use all your wisdom to teach and
instruct each other. With thankful hearts,
sing psalms, hymns, and spiritual songs to God.

COLOSSIANS 3:16 CEV

Roadblocks

Let your hope make you glad.
Be patient in time of trouble
and never stop praying.
ROMANS 12:12 CEV

Detours are frustrating. They make us late and disrupt our plans. One way to manage detours effectively is to anticipate them and plan accordingly. Leaving a few minutes earlier can minimize frustration when we are stopped by a train. Bringing an extra snack can stave off hunger when mealtime is delayed. Preparing for trouble eliminates the surprise, and often the frustration, that comes with roadblocks.

As Jesus said good-bye to His disciples, He prepared them for trouble: "I have told you all this so that you may have peace in me. Here on earth you will have many trials and sorrows. But take heart, because I have overcome the world" (John 16:33 NLT). Carrying Jesus' words with us in an attitude of prayer is the most effective way to cope with life's inevitable roadblocks.

"Be prepared." The old scouting motto is a good one for the Christian life as well. While we can't expect our journeys to always be smooth and without roadblocks, we can have peace of mind that Christ will help us persevere, especially when we are well-prepared. These Bible verses outline many of the qualities that help prepare us for life's journey.

▶ Endurance
▶ Strength
▶ Character
▶ Confidence
▶ Hope of salvation
▶ Perseverance
▶ Praise

Next to each quality, write down some of the ways they have been displayed in your life recently. To help memorize the following verses, create a picture for each of them in your mind. For example, you might envision lifting a weight with the word *endurance* on it, or use your imagination to see God defending you as He did the Israelites in Exodus. These images will help the words come alive.

*And endurance develops strength
of character, and character strengthens
our confident hope of salvation.*
ROMANS 5:4 NLT

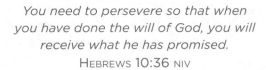

*You need to persevere so that when
you have done the will of God, you will
receive what he has promised.*
HEBREWS 10:36 NIV

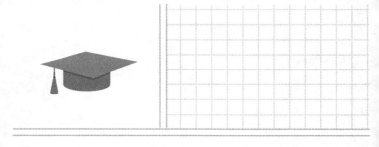

The Lord is my strength and my defense;
he has become my salvation. He is my God,
and I will praise him, my father's God,
and I will exalt him.

Exodus 15:2 NIV

Perception

Imagine you're in a dark forest, surrounded by trees and tall, growing weeds. Nothing makes sense, and the way seems unclear. Now imagine riding in an airplane, seven or eight thousand feet above the ground. Ahhh. . .it's easier to see now. The dark forest has a beginning, a middle, and an end. There is an order to things. From the air, the same forest seems far more navigable.

When we look at life from the depth of our troubles, we become discouraged, hopeless, and afraid. On the other hand, when we "fix our gaze on things that cannot be seen," we are propelled by hope to rise above our circumstances.

No matter how bleak the view before you, ask your Father to give you His perspective. The way will seem far clearer.

Abraham Lincoln said, "We can complain because rose bushes have thorns, or rejoice because thorn bushes have roses." Same rose, but the perspective is far different. A change in perspective changes our thinking, and when our thinking changes, our feelings and behaviors will as well.

Suffering often brings shame, but Peter calls us to see it as a privilege. Paul sees his weakness as a thorn in his side, but God views it as a vehicle for Christ's strength and power. In Matthew, Jesus says our eyes (perspective) provide a window for our body. When we see circumstances from God's perspective, we have all the light we need.

As you memorize the following verses, take a moment to write down two or three difficult things you are facing right now. How can you see your circumstances from an alternative perspective? Pray that God would help you to focus on the roses instead of the thorns.

*But it is no shame to suffer for being
a Christian. Praise God for the privilege
of being called by his name!*
1 PETER 4:16 NLT

*But he said to me, "My grace is sufficient
for you, for my power is made perfect in
weakness." Therefore I will boast all the
more gladly about my weaknesses,
so that Christ's power may rest on me.*
2 CORINTHIANS 12:9 NIV

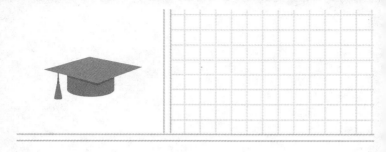

Your eyes are like a window for your body.
When they are good, you have
all the light you need.

MATTHEW 6:22 CEV

Hope

Such things were written in the Scriptures long ago to teach us. And the Scriptures give us hope and encouragement as we wait patiently for God's promises to be fulfilled.

ROMANS 15:4 NLT

Abraham and Sarah longed for a son.

God made a promise.

But as the years passed, the once-shiny hope grew tarnished by an empty, barren womb. As his wife's hope wavered, surely at times Abraham wondered if God would be true to His word. Yet Romans tells us, "'Abraham believed God, and it was credited to him as righteousness'" (Romans 4:3 NIV). For years and years, Abraham and Sarah waited and clung, though sometimes only barely, to the promise of descendants that would outnumber the sands on the seashore. However Genesis 21:1 tells us that God kept His word.

Waiting is hard. It tries our patience and can leave us feeling discouraged. But just like Sarah and Abraham, we can believe God and rest in the truth and fulfillment of His word, no matter how long the wait.

What is this world coming to? Spending thirty minutes watching the evening news or perusing the latest newspaper headlines is enough to leave us feeling hopeless and fearful. War, death, destruction, and oppression seem to be far more prevalent than peace, joy, and harmony.

True, the world is filled with darkness. But we can rest firmly on the truth of His promises. He *is* all-powerful. He *will* destroy the power of death. He *will* wipe away all our tears. We will not be insulted! Our Redeemer lives, and He *will* return to us.

How can you cling more tightly to this hope today? Pray this prayer as you memorize His Word:

All-Powerful Father,

When my soul grows weary with waiting, help me to lean on the truth of Your promises. Give me strength for the waiting, help me rely on You. In Jesus' precious and holy name I pray. Amen.

*The Lord All-Powerful will destroy the power
of death and wipe away all tears. No longer
will his people be insulted everywhere.
The Lord has spoken!*
ISAIAH 25:8 CEV

❖

*"But as for me, I know that my Redeemer lives,
and he will stand upon the earth at last."*
JOB 19:25 NLT

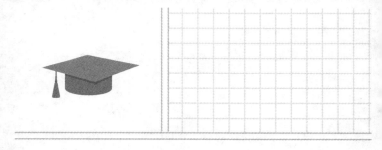

Praise God, the Father of our Lord Jesus Christ.
God is so good, and by raising Jesus from death,
he has given us new life and a hope that lives on.

1 PETER 1:3 CEV

God's Phone Number

"Call to me and I will answer you and tell you great and unsearchable things you do not know."
JEREMIAH 33:3 NIV

What did we do without cell phones? It's hard to remember that once upon a time, folks depended on men with horses to transmit important information. While technology does enable us to be in communication with one another 24/7, we still have to dial a number, make the call, send the e-mail or text, and wait for the response.

Long before this technology was developed, God instituted a vehicle for communication with Him that never has a bad connection. Prayer means the call can never be dropped, the service is never spotty.

We never have to wait for Him to be available or wonder when He will return our call. Prayer enables us to communicate directly, immediately, and powerfully. Keep your soul in communication with Him at all times. He has much to tell you!

The disciples were with Jesus all the time. What must they have thought when they saw Him wake early in the morning to spend time with His Father or watched Him steal away from the crowds? They no doubt longed to have the open communication with God that Jesus did.

Jesus patiently instructed them, because prayer is something we must learn. It doesn't always come naturally. In fact, we probably make it far too complicated. This causes us to avoid it and miss valuable time of connection, love, and support with our Lord. In Matthew 6:9–13, Jesus gives the disciples and us some simple guidelines for prayer:

- Ask in His name.
- Ask for His will.
- Trust Him to provide.
- Receive and offer forgiveness.

Like any skill, we become better at prayer with practice. As you memorize these scriptures, turn to God in prayer.

"Until now you have not asked for anything in my name. Ask and you will receive, and your joy will be complete."

JOHN 16:24 NIV

"I also tell you this: If two of you agree here on earth concerning anything you ask, my Father in heaven will do it for you. For where two or three gather together as my followers, I am there among them."

MATTHEW 18:19–20 NLT

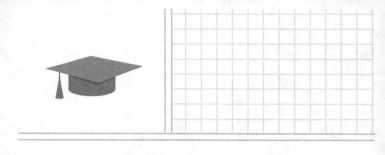

*Lord All-Powerful, you are greater
than all others. No one is like you,
and you alone are God.
Everything we have heard about you is true.*

2 Samuel 7:22 CEV

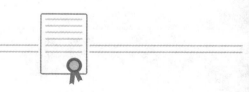

God Lights the Way

*Your word is a lamp to guide my feet
and a light for my path.*
PSALM 119:105 NLT

God freed the Israelites from Egypt and assured them of their destination—the Promised Land. The journey was long. They would need provisions. Since there was more than one path, the way was not clear. The Lord provided a guiding cloud by day and a pillar of fire by night (see Exodus 13:21–22). To sustain them physically, He provided manna. Manna was nourishing and plentiful, but only available to them in the quantities they needed in the moment. If they tried to save it for another day, it would rot.

We often want God to provide a roadmap with a clear destination and give us plenty of notice about the next step. However, He would much rather have us learn, like the Israelites, to depend on Him for each step. God promises to give you what you need in the very next moment. You can trust Him each step of the way.

What is God's will for my life? Trying to make the right decision can be paralyzing. We become so fearful of taking a wrong turn or a major misstep that we just stand in place.

Our ultimate destination is heaven—we know that. So why are there so many opportunities to wander along the way? God has much to teach us during the journey. Learning God's will for our lives is a process. It involves tuning into the Holy Spirit, day by day, listening to the Lord's guidance, and taking one step at a time.

To aid your memory of these verses, draw a path on a piece of paper. Line the path by copying down the following verses in or along the way. If you feel like being creative, add some color and scenery to your map. In the days and months that follow, refer to your map often, in prayer, to remind you of God's wonderful plans for your life.

"For I know the plans I have for you,"
says the LORD. "They are plans for good and not
for disaster, to give you a future and a hope."
JEREMIAH 29:11 NLT

We make our own plans, but the Lord
decides where we will go.
PROVERBS 16:9 CEV

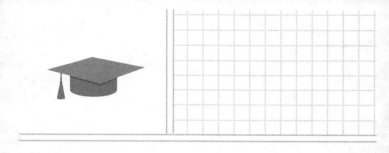

Trust in the Lord with all your heart;
do not depend on your own understanding.
Seek his will in all you do, and he will
show you which path to take.

<small>PROVERBS 3:5-6 NLT</small>

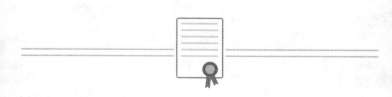

Giving Out of Need

But don't forget to help others and to share your possessions with them. This too is like offering a sacrifice that pleases God.
HEBREWS 13:16 CEV

Jesus was a man of strong opinions. One day He was in the temple talking about the teachers of the Law of Moses. Later, He watched as people brought their gifts to the temple. Is it possible, as the rich walked by, that they hoped Jesus would notice their generosity? Surely the widow wasn't expecting to be recognized by the Master, but she was the one Jesus honored. The widow, who put in barely a few pennies, was praised for her generosity. She gave out of her need, while the rich gave out of their abundance. The sacrifice, the trust, and the heart were what honored God.

Our ability to give generously indicates our faith and reliance on Him and becomes a sacrifice that pleases God. Look for big and small ways to give to others—give them your thanks and praise, share possessions, and open your home. Jesus longs to bless you for your generosity.

The quote "we make a living by what we get; we make a life by what we give" has been attributed to Winston Churchill. Giving blesses us, and in Luke 6:38, Jesus says that we will receive in the same manner we give. There are so many reasons to give generously and freely. Often, giving of our time can be as sacrificial as giving of our finances.

Setting aside the time to memorize scripture is one way to give back to Him. Sharing time with another person is a way of giving away His blessings to another.

Partner with a friend to memorize the following verses. Take turns repeating the lines to each other. Then look for ways the two of you can give.

And I have been a constant example of how you can help those in need by working hard. You should remember the words of the Lord Jesus: "It is more blessed to give than to receive."

ACTS 20:35 NLT

You obey the law of Christ when you offer each other a helping hand.

GALATIANS 6:2 CEV

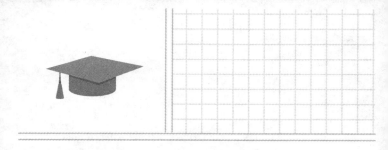

Each of you should give what you have decided in your heart to give, not reluctantly or under compulsion, for God loves a cheerful giver.

2 Corinthians 9:7 NIV

A Time to Speak, a Time Not To

Even fools are thought wise when they keep silent; with their mouths shut, they seem intelligent.

PROVERBS 17:28 NLT

Have you ever thought of the perfect comeback, days after the conversation occurred?

We sometimes struggle to think of the right thing to say in the moment and even feel foolish for keeping our mouths shut. However, Ecclesiastes 3:7 says there is a time for speaking and a time to be quiet. Jesus modeled this throughout His ministry. He was an amazing communicator who spoke confidently and boldly when the time was right and, when necessary, remained silent, even when many of us would have cried out to defend ourselves.

Depending on the moment, a well-timed silence can be far more powerful than a lengthy speech. In fact, Proverbs says that silence can make even foolish people appear wise! Pray that God would show you how to discern when to speak and when to remain silent.

Our words reveal a lot about us. A certain accent or dialect can indicate what part of the world we're from, even among English speakers in the US. Our words can reflect our moods, our attitudes, our level of education, and our regard for others. When we speak boldly and confidently, people often listen to us and consider us with respect. When we speak quietly and with reserve, people might assume we don't know what we're talking about.

It's important to choose our words—and the way we say them—very carefully. When people ask us questions, this shows us they are eager to hear what we have to say. The Bible says to be prepared when someone "asks us about our hope." Your answer is your testimony—your own personal story of the difference God has made in your life. It doesn't have to be long—in fact, you could tell your whole story in just a few sentences.

If you've never done so, try writing out a couple different versions of your testimony. Weave in the following verses, so that you will always be ready to speak wisely when asked about your hope.

Always be ready to give an answer when someone asks you about your hope.
1 Peter 3:15 cev

───────◆───────

May the words of my mouth and the meditation of my heart be pleasing to you, O Lord, my rock and my redeemer.
Psalm 19:14 nlt

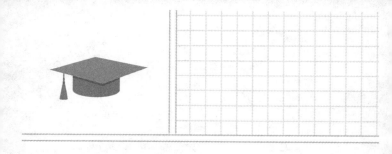

*Those who guard their lips preserve
their lives, but those who speak
rashly will come to ruin.*

PROVERBS 13:3 NIV

Loving Others

All that the Law says can be summed up in the command to love others as much as you love yourself.

GALATIANS 5:14 CEV

When Jesus was a boy of about six or seven, He likely attended a school for young Jewish males, called bet sefer, "house of the book." There He would have memorized the first five books of the Bible, the Torah, with its complicated do's and don'ts, rights and wrongs, and rules for living. Wouldn't it have been tempting to try and condense them into fewer words?

In the New Testament, Jesus does this. Can you imagine Him speaking to the Jews? "You know how you took all those years to memorize Torah? Well, I can sum it up in for you in four simple words: *Love God; love others.*"

The Bible is filled with many details and stories. But Jesus brought radical simplicity to their complexity. "All the law says" He summed up in one simple phrase: "Love God; love others." It's that simple. Do that and you can't fail.

Sometimes we humans have a tendency to make things too complicated. Take memory, for example. The idea of memorizing a passage or series of verses seems so overwhelming, we talk ourselves out of it before we even start.

Often, half the battle to successful memorization is convincing yourself you can do it.

One simple tool for memorization is repetition. The more we repeat words over and over, the more likely they are to take hold in our memory. Copy the following verses onto index cards to carry with you. Try to read them, out loud, four to five times every day for five days. After you read them, close your eyes and try to say the words from memory. Take a moment to picture each word in your mind. Commit to making scripture memory a habit. You will be surprised at how simple it can become.

*Therefore, accept each other just as Christ
has accepted you so that God
will be given glory.*
ROMANS 15:7 NLT

---

*Dear friends, let us love one another,
for love comes from God. Everyone who loves
has been born of God and knows God.
Whoever does not love does not know
God, because God is love.*
1 JOHN 4:7–8 NIV

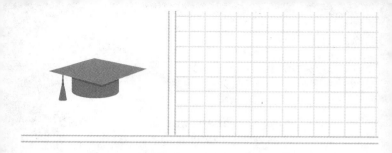

"*So now I am giving you a new commandment:*
Love each other. Just as I have loved you,
you should love each other."

JOHN 13:34 NLT

Power to Obey

*For God is working in you,
giving you the desire and the power
to do what pleases him.*

PHILIPPIANS 2:13 NLT

In the eighteenth and nineteenth centuries, many North Americans depended on their communities to do together what a family could not do alone— build a barn. Still today, the Amish community is known for its ability to erect a barn in just one or two days. When many hands work together, there is incredible strength and power!

Trying to be obedient on our own is like trying to build a barn by ourselves. Impossible. The only way we can accomplish this incredible feat is through the hand of the Father, the Son, and the Holy Spirit. When we depend on our own desire and power, we are inadequate. The task becomes monumental and ultimately impossible. But when we avail ourselves of God's power, we can accomplish great things!

Let His power work through you to do the impossible.

Have you ever wondered why phone numbers (without area codes) are seven numbers long? In the 1950s, psychologists discovered the "magical number seven" to be about the number of digits or items that human beings can immediately retain. This is called the brain's "working memory." Too much beyond seven and our working memory becomes maxed out. To help your scripture memory be more effective, try memorizing just seven words or syllables at a time. You might copy these seven items over, from memory, several times, before adding the next seven.

For example, to memorize 1 John 5:3, you would memorize, then write from memory:

We show our love for God by. . .

The next few words have more syllables, so just do seven syllables:

Obeying his commandments. . .

Finally, add the last seven words:

And they are not hard to follow.

Breaking verses up into manageable chunks coincides naturally with the brain's working memory to help God's Word become a permanent fixture in your brain!

We show our love for God by obeying his commandments, and they are not hard to follow.

1 JOHN 5:3 CEV

Know therefore that the LORD your God is God; he is the faithful God, keeping his covenant of love to a thousand generations of those who love him and keep his commandments.

DEUTERONOMY 7:9 NIV

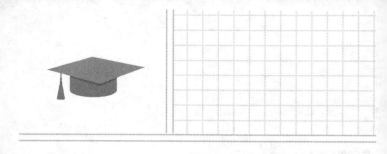

*We demolish arguments and every pretension
that sets itself up against the knowledge
of God, and we take captive every thought
to make it obedient to Christ.*

2 CORINTHIANS 10:5 NIV

Trusting God

Then he passed in front of Moses and called out, "I am the LORD God. I am merciful and very patient with my people. I show great love, and I can be trusted."

EXODUS 34:6 CEV

We could consider the book of Exodus Moses' memoir—a compelling account of his life story. When he was a baby, Moses' mother abandoned him in desperation. After a daring rescue, he was raised in an opulent palace. Then he committed murder and was exiled to the wilderness. When it all seemed hopeless, God appeared and called him by name: "Moses! I AM! I am MERCIFUL, PATIENT. I show great love. I CAN BE TRUSTED!"

Would it make a difference for you if God appeared in a burning bush and told you by His own tongue that He could be trusted?

Just like Moses, we wander. Life takes us far from where we thought we'd be. But through it all, no matter what, we serve a God who can be trusted.

How will you trust Him today?

Most of us haven't written our own memoirs, but keeping a spiritual journal is a way of recounting the stories of God's work in our lives. It allows us to capture thoughts on paper and to keep a record of growth. It can also help us remember important truths we don't want to forget. The written word becomes a lasting and tangible reminder, long after our immediate recall fades.

When the Israelites were discouraged, they recounted God's faithfulness to one another. They told the stories, over and over again, of how God has rescued them from slavery, how He had conquered the Egyptians and saved His people from death and destruction.

How has God proven Himself trustworthy in your life? What are the stories you can tell? Can you recount His blessings? Start keeping a journal and write out the stories of the many ways He has blessed you. When you begin to wonder if you can trust Him, go back to your memoir. He has surely done great things, and He will again!

I am counting on the LORD; yes, I am counting on him. I have put my hope in his word.
PSALM 130:5 NLT

Some trust in chariots and some in horses, but we trust in the name of the LORD our God.
PSALM 20:7 NIV

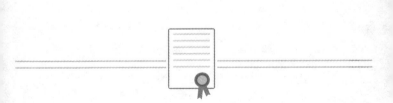

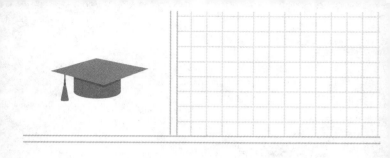

Don't fall into the trap of being a coward—
trust the LORD, and you will be safe.

PROVERBS 29:25 CEV

The Holy Spirit

*But the Holy Spirit produces this
kind of fruit in our lives: love, joy,
peace, patience, kindness, goodness,
faithfulness, gentleness, and self-control.
There is no law against these things!*
GALATIANS 5:22–23 NLT

In Matthew 7:17, Jesus said a good tree produces good fruit and a bad tree produces bad fruit. In John 15:5, He uses the image of a vine to explain how we are connected to Him and reminds us that we have to be pruned in order to grow. This growth occurs through the power of the Holy Spirit. In Matthew 7:20 Jesus says the fruit we bear on the outside is a clear indication of what is happening inside our lives. Yielding ourselves to the Holy Spirit enables us to grow and allows others to recognize us as His offspring.

When Jesus left earth, He gave the disciples (and us) a powerful gift to help with growth. The Holy Spirit enables all Christians to do what seems impossible without Him.

Praise God for this gift!

In John 16:5–15, Jesus promises the disciples (and us) the gift of the Holy Spirit.

The Holy Spirit plays an essential role in our lives as believers, enabling us to do through Him what we cannot do on our own. Look up the following verses to determine some of the functions of the Holy Spirit:

- ▶ John 15:8–11
- ▶ John 15:26–27
- ▶ John 14:26
- ▶ Romans 8:14
- ▶ Romans 8:26
- ▶ Galatians 5:16, 18
- ▶ 1 Corinthians 2:6–14
- ▶ 2 Timothy 3:16–17

What role does the Spirit play in your life? Memorizing the following verses will help remind you of this gift:

*The Lord and the Spirit are one and the same,
and the Lord's Spirit sets us free.*
2 Corinthians 3:17 cev

---

*Yet God raised Jesus to life! God's Spirit
now lives in you, and he will raise you
to life by his Spirit.*
Romans 8:11 cev

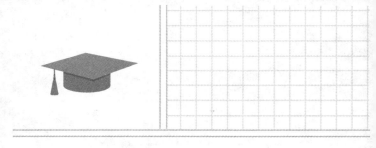

*But the Holy Spirit will come and help you,
because the Father will send the Spirit
to take my place. The Spirit will teach
you everything and will remind you of
what I said while I was with you.*

JOHN 14:26 CEV

Standing Out

Don't copy the behavior and customs of this world, but let God transform you into a new person by changing the way you think. Then you will learn to know God's will for you, which is good and pleasing and perfect.

ROMANS 12:2 NLT

Joe didn't like to stand out. Plain vanilla was his favorite ice cream. White T-shirts and blue jeans were his wardrobe. If there was anything flashy or obvious about Joe, he hid it well. Except—Joe was different. He was quiet when others were loud and seeking attention. He paused to pray before he ate his meals. He stopped to lend a hand to strangers, and he always seemed to be giving something away. As hard as he tried to blend in, Joe couldn't help but stand out, because he had learned not to copy the behavior and customs of the world. Joe's love for God's Word had changed Joe's thoughts, and over time he learned God's good, pleasing, and perfect will for his life.

When you live for God, you will be transformed into a new person—one who stands out to others for all the right reasons.

"Dress for success."

"The clothes make the man."

"She's dressed to kill."

Our clothing says a lot about us. Of course, a person could always be a wolf in sheep's clothing, but what we wear generally says a lot about the person inside. The colors we choose send a message. After all, we know red is a good color for a power tie and purple is the color of royalty. Uniforms carry with them an air of authority, while ragged, dirty clothes tell another story.

We typically put a lot of thought into our physical wardrobes. But what about our spiritual wardrobes? What do these verses tell us about how to clothe ourselves spiritually?

Therefore, as God's chosen people, holy and dearly loved, clothe yourselves with compassion, kindness, humility, gentleness and patience.

COLOSSIANS 3:12 NIV

Make your light shine, so that others will see the good that you do and will praise your Father in heaven.

MATTHEW 5:16 CEV

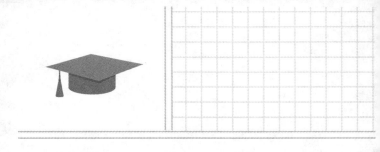

For once you were full of darkness,
but now you have light from the Lord.
So live as people of light!

Ephesians 5:8 NLT

The Gift of Forgiveness

So now there is no condemnation
for those who belong to Christ Jesus.
And because you belong to him,
the power of the life-giving Spirit
has freed you from the power
of sin that leads to death.

ROMANS 8:1–2 NLT

If Satan can't discourage us enough to get us to ignore God completely, he tries another way. He tries to cover us with shame—shame of our past mistakes, sins, and failures. If he can keep us trapped in shame, we will be less effective for God's kingdom. Living in condemnation is like trying to walk around with a ball and chain at our ankle. But Paul brings us the good news that, no matter what we've done, there is no condemnation in Christ! Corrie ten Boom said it's as if God throws our sins into the deepest ocean, then places a "no fishing" sign there.

Do you belong to Christ? This is the key to feeling no condemnation. You are promised the "life-giving" Spirit, which brings freedom from sin. Thanks be to God for His indescribable gift!

It has been said that failing to forgive others is like swallowing poison and hoping the other person will die. We first have to receive God's forgiveness in order to give it to others. Then we have to forgive ourselves. Once we have truly received this gift, we are then free to share it with others. Meditate on the following verses. As you do so, see if you can write out a definition of the following:

- ▶ Redemption
- ▶ Forgiveness
- ▶ Grace
- ▶ Trust
- ▶ Confession
- ▶ Kindness
- ▶ Tenderheartedness

Is there anything holding you back from receiving God's forgiveness? Have you forgiven yourself—agreed with God about your sin? What holds you back from forgiving others? Write down each sin you are holding onto that may feel like a ball and chain. Ask for God's forgiveness, then blot each out, throw it away, or burn it in a fire. Agree with God that your sins are forgiven and there is no longer any condemnation!

*In him we have redemption through his blood,
the forgiveness of sins, in accordance with
the riches of God's grace.*
EPHESIANS 1:7 NIV

*But if we confess our sins to God,
he can always be trusted to forgive
us and take our sins away.*
1 JOHN 1:9 CEV

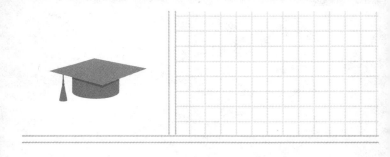

*Instead, be kind to each other,
tenderhearted, forgiving one another,
just as God through Christ has forgiven you.*

EPHESIANS 4:32 NLT

God's Comfort

*Do you not know? Have you not heard? The L*ORD *is the everlasting God, the Creator of the ends of the earth. He will not grow tired or weary, and his understanding no one can fathom.*
ISAIAH 40:28 NIV

Elijah was exhausted. He had grown so weary in his ministry that he finally gave in. He eventually sat under a broom tree and prayed for God to take his life. Elijah surely was physically tired, but scripture is clear that he was emotionally tired as well, even depressed. Depression is often shown by a lack of hope, and Elijah's prayer for God to take his life is certainly an indication he lacked hope that things would get any better.

God sent an angel to minister to Elijah, helping him sleep and eat and recover. The ministering angel brought great comfort to Elijah and refreshed and renewed him.

Life is hard for all of us, and it is normal to feel hopeless from time to time. However, like Elijah, God will minister to us and refresh us and renew us when we cry out to Him.

Eating right, exercising, and getting enough sleep are three very basic ways we can take care of ourselves. Elijah's story reminds us that God cares deeply about our physical needs and understands that we will run out of strength from time to time. Studies show that exercising three times a week for about thirty minutes a day can be just as effective as medication in relieving some of the symptoms of depression. This is hard to believe, but it is good evidence that maintaining good physical habits can profoundly impact our mental functioning.

Developing good spiritual health habits is even more important. The internal spiritual disciplines include prayer, meditation, fasting, and Bible study. These disciplines help maintain our spiritual fitness and, just like physical exercise, prepare us to perform our spiritual tasks such as service, evangelism, and teaching to the best of our abilities.

Make spiritual disciplines a priority and receive the comfort God's Word provides.

The name of the LORD is a strong fortress;
the godly run to him and are safe.
PROVERBS 18:10 NLT

Because of the LORD's great love we
are not consumed, for his compassions
never fail. They are new every morning;
great is your faithfulness.
LAMENTATIONS 3:22–23 NIV

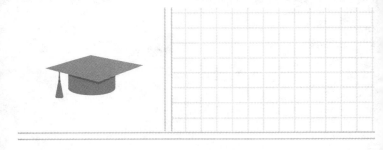

*How precious are your thoughts about me,
O God. They cannot be numbered! I can't even
count them; they outnumber the grains of sand!
And when I wake up, you are still with me!*

PSALM 139:17–18 NLT

The Value of Perseverance

God blesses those who patiently endure testing and temptation. Afterward they will receive the crown of life that God has promised to those who love him.

JAMES 1:12 NLT

When we are really hungry, anything sounds good, even rich and fluffy desserts. Our brains tell us that we need to eat our meat and vegetables first, but to an empty stomach, the sweetness and sugar can be irresistible. However, most of us wouldn't consider making dessert first a habit. Can you imagine the problems it would create? Failing to leave room for the food that matters—the healthy proteins, fats, and carbohydrates our bodies need to run efficiently—leaves us sick and flabby.

The wise person takes a peek at the dessert, but resists, knowing better than to waste nutrition on empty calories and instead choosing the wiser course that blesses the body with health and strength. And so it is with temptation and our spiritual lives. Giving in to temptation is like accepting empty calories. They will fill, but only temporarily. Resisting temptation allows us to leave room for what really matters—God's precious and promised crown of life.

In John 8:44 (NIV), Jesus says that Satan is the "father of lies." Jesus faced Satan and his lies head on after forty days of fasting in the desert (see Matthew 4). Having gone without food for more than a month, Jesus was vulnerable, and He was tempted. But Jesus stood firm and did not sin. He refused the devil's temptation by countering the lies with His Father's truth.

When we give in to temptation, we are essentially telling Satan that we agree with his lies. Look up the following verses and contrast Satan's lies with God's truth:

- ▶ Matthew 4:3–4
- ▶ Matthew 4:6–7
- ▶ Matthew 4:9–10

You probably have never fasted for forty days; however, there are other things that might leave you vulnerable. When are you most vulnerable? Which lies does Satan tempt you with? Search the Bible for truths that counteract these lies and commit them to memory. Then you will be equipped, like Jesus, to stand firm against the devil's flimsy schemes.

*But those who trust in the L*ORD *will find new strength. They will soar high on wings like eagles. They will run and not grow weary. They will walk and not faint.*
ISAIAH 40:31 NLT

Don't be afraid, for I am with you. Don't be discouraged, for I am your God. I will strengthen you and help you. I will hold you up with my victorious right hand.
ISAIAH 41:10 NLT

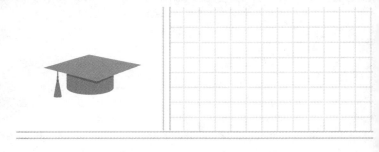

The Spirit will show you what is true.
The people of this world cannot accept
the Spirit, because they don't see or know him.
But you know the Spirit, who is with you
and will keep on living in you.

JOHN 14:17 CEV

God's Armor

*Finally, let the mighty strength
of the Lord make you strong.
Put on all the armor that God gives,
so you can defend yourself
against the devil's tricks.*

EPHESIANS 6:10–11 CEV

1 Samuel 17 tells the incredible story of how young David defeated the nine-foot bully, Goliath. For over a month, Goliath stood, covered in heavy armor, and used his size and his enormous voice to taunt God's people. Can you imagine the humiliation? They must have had terribly mixed feelings. On the one hand, they desperately wanted the bullying to stop, but on the other hand, fear drained the strength from their bodies.

Then along came David, who was only a boy. Goliath's taunting infuriated him. Someone had to put a stop to it. How desperate Saul must have been to agree to allow David to face the giant. He offered David the only thing he could—his own armor. David rejected Saul's armor because ultimately he knew he did not need man's armor—he needed God's. Then, with God's strength, he defeated the giant.

How can God's armor help you face your bullies?

Like Goliath, Satan stands tall and tries to bully and taunt us. Like David, we have the power to resist Satan's lies with the strength of God's armor (see 1 Samuel 17:47). Yes, Satan has power here on earth. But it is limited and doesn't hold a candle to the strength God provides.

Look at the following verses and contrast what Satan tries to tell us with the truth of God's Word:

Instead of fear and timidity, we have a spirit of power, love, and self-discipline.

For God has not given us a spirit of fear and timidity, but of power, love, and self-discipline.
2 TIMOTHY 1:7 NLT

Instead of being entangled by sin, we are free to run when we fix our eyes on Jesus and follow His path.

Therefore, since we are surrounded by such a great cloud of witnesses, let us throw off everything that hinders and the sin that so easily entangles. And let us run with perseverance the race marked out for us, fixing our eyes on Jesus, the pioneer and perfecter of faith. For the joy set before him he endured the cross, scorning its shame, and sat down at the right hand of the throne of God.
HEBREWS 12:1–2 NIV

When you memorize these verses, highlight all the words that indicate the strength God gives you.

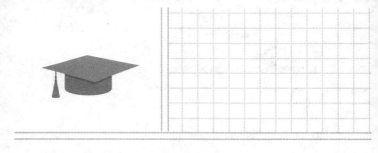

Each time he said, "My grace is all you need. My power works best in weakness." So now I am glad to boast about my weaknesses, so that the power of Christ can work through me.

2 Corinthians 12:9 NLT

Simple Living

Jesus replied, "If you want to be perfect, go sell everything you own! Give the money to the poor, and you will have riches in heaven. Then come and be my follower." When the young man heard this, he was sad, because he was very rich.

MATTHEW 19:21-22 CEV

The rich man of Matthew 19 must have felt pretty good about himself. When he asked Jesus, "What good thing must I do to have eternal life?" he was looking for affirmation, not an honest answer. Jesus told him to follow the commandments, and the rich man gave a thumbs up. "What else?" he asked (vv. 16–20 CEV).

Jesus stopped him in his tracks. "Okay, you want to be perfect? Sell all your stuff and give the money to the poor, then follow me." The man was heartbroken. He had a lot of stuff and was looking for one more thing to add to his "to do for good" list—not a radical life transformation.

When we merely try to follow commandments but miss the core of Jesus' message, we fall short. Jesus wants our whole hearts.

It's difficult to follow Him if your heart is tied to earthly things.

The only way to combat this is to become a seeker of simplicity. Here are a few ways to live a more simple life. Can you think of others?

▶ Resist signing up for e-mails that only clutter your inbox (and constantly invite you to spend more money). Every few months, go through your e-mails and unsubscribe from anything that tries to sell you something or feels like clutter.

▶ Regularly go through your closets and drawers. Sell or donate the things that are gathering dust.

▶ Instead of giving tangible gifts to others, give the gift of a memory. Take a friend out for a special dinner or plan a day-long outing at the zoo. The memories will last far longer than the stuff.

▶ Make a twenty-four-hour rule for purchases. Resist the urge to impulse buy anything. For needed items, do your research and know what you want before you shop. For wanted items, wait a day or two. Will this add or subtract from your life? How much money and time will you need to maintain it? Will it provide more memories or merely obligations?

Pray through the following verses as you commit them to memory. What does God have to say about the philosophy that "more is more?"

A simple meal with love is better than a feast where there is hatred.
PROVERBS 15:17 CEV

No, O people, the LORD has told you what is good, and this is what he requires of you: to do what is right, to love mercy, and to walk humbly with your God.
MICAH 6:8 NLT

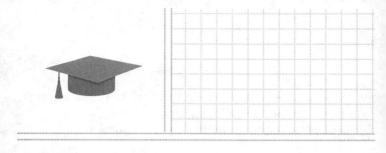

Don't store up treasures on earth! Moths and rust can destroy them, and thieves can break in and steal them. Instead, store up your treasures in heaven, where moths and rust cannot destroy them, and thieves cannot break in and steal them. Your heart will always be where your treasure is.

MATTHEW 6:19–21 CEV

Doing the Right Thing

*But you, man of God, flee from all this,
and pursue righteousness, godliness,
faith, love, endurance and gentleness.*

1 TIMOTHY 6:11 NIV

Joseph had many things that we might envy. He was handsome, intelligent, and lived in a palace. On top of that, the wife of Potiphar himself propositioned him—she offered him sex with no strings attached.

Joseph didn't stick around to flirt with disaster—he did what the Bible says we should do when tempted to do wrong—he escaped. For Joseph, doing the right thing had its consequences. He was imprisoned and forgotten. But God used the experience to demonstrate His love and power and to save a nation. If Joseph had done the wrong thing, we probably never would have known his story.

Don't be ashamed by temptation; after all, everyone is tempted. But instead of giving in, take it to God—He will show you how to do the right thing.

Psalm 139:14 (NIV) reminds us that we are "fearfully and wonderfully made." Our five senses allow us to see, hear, smell, taste, and touch the world around us, and unless we have lost one of those abilities, we often take this miracle for granted. When we use all of our senses to connect with our experiences, they become more ingrained in our brains. As you work toward memorizing these verses, think of ways you can engage all five of your senses. Galatians 6:9 paints a beautiful picture of reaping a harvest of blessing. Find or draw a cornucopia and fill it with good-smelling fruits and vegetables. Say the verses aloud or listen to someone else read them. Print them out and post them on your wall so you can see them.

What are other ways you can "taste and see that the Lord is good" (Psalm 34:8 NIV)?

So let's not get tired of doing what is good.
At just the right time we will reap a harvest
of blessing if we don't give up.
GALATIANS 6:9 NLT

But now that you have been set free
from sin and have become slaves of God,
the benefit you reap leads to holiness,
and the result is eternal life.
ROMANS 6:22 NIV

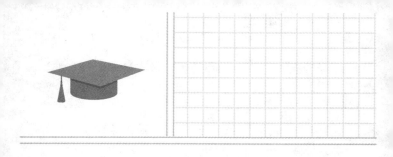

Christ gives me the strength to face anything.

PHILIPPIANS 4:13 CEV

Gifts for Others

*A spiritual gift is given to each of us
so we can help each other.*
1 CORINTHIANS 12:7 NLT

The Holy Spirit is alive in you! In 1 Corinthians, Paul teaches that the Spirit gives us different gifts so we can help one another. Some of us have the gift of wisdom, others have special knowledge or mercy. Some believers are blessed with a great faith, and others are able to heal or teach.

How do you know where your gifts are? One simple way is to practice. Try different things. What do you enjoy doing? Do others affirm these things in you? Do you feel energized by what you are doing? If you are serving the Lord and are enjoying it, this could very well be your area of giftedness. Make finding and using your spiritual gifts a lifelong pursuit, and be sure to always use them to help others.

God has so many gifts He wants to give you. Receive them. Believe they are for you. Creating visual aids can help God's Word be more implanted in your brain. Here are some ideas:

▸ Go through old magazines or print out pictures from the Internet that remind you of words in the following verses. Create a collage or scrapbook to help you recall these important words.

▸ Type the words to your verses out in large print. Print them, and cut them apart. Then see if you can fit them together in order.

▸ Create flash cards.

▸ Write them with a dry-erase marker on your bathroom mirror.

Can you think of other creative ways to incorporate these verses into your daily life?

*From his abundance we have all received
one gracious blessing after another.*
JOHN 1:16 NLT

*Every good and perfect gift comes down from
the Father who created all the lights
in the heavens. He is always the same
and never makes dark shadows by changing.*
JAMES 1:17 CEV

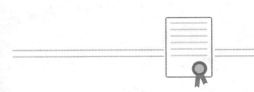

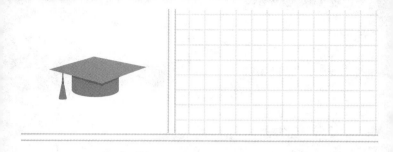

*By his divine power, God has given us everything
we need for living a godly life. We have received
all of this by coming to know him, the one who
called us to himself by means of his marvelous
glory and excellence.*

2 PETER 1:3 NLT

Fight or Flight

Give all your worries and cares to God, for he cares about you.
1 PETER 5:7 NLT

One of the miracles of the human body is the fight-or-flight response. When our brains perceive life-threatening danger, all nonessential functions of our bodies shut down. Our heart rates increase, our breathing becomes shallow, our senses are quickened. We are flooded with stress chemicals so that every part of us is alert and aware, prepared to stay and fight or flee for our lives. Although this is a very useful physiological response to stress, it unfortunately can happen in ordinary situations like traffic jams and long lines at the bank. As a result, many of us live in a perpetual state of readiness, even though there is no real danger. Another name for this false fear is anxiety. Anxiety is burdensome, uncomfortable, and even dangerous because of the stress it places on our bodies.

God's Word has some amazingly practical advice to manage anxiety. First and foremost— give it to God. He cares for you.

Ever had a night when you couldn't sleep? 1 Samuel 16 tells of Saul's anxiety. In his case, he was tormented by an evil spirit that kept him awake and anxious. He eventually called for David to come and play the harp for him. It was the only thing that would soothe his troubled soul. Anxiety can keep us up at night as well. One way we can manage anxiety more effectively is to meditate on God's Word. Here are some ways to incorporate scripture memory into your sleepless nights:

▸ Try to think of a name or attribute of God for every letter of the alphabet.

▸ Pray for every single member of your family by name.

▸ Listen to praise music that incorporates scripture.

▸ Recite the following verses over and over until God's peace settles your soul.

Then Jesus said, "Come to me, all of you who are weary and carry heavy burdens, and I will give you rest."

MATTHEW 11:28 NLT

"So don't worry about tomorrow, for tomorrow will bring its own worries. Today's trouble is enough for today."

MATTHEW 6:34 NLT

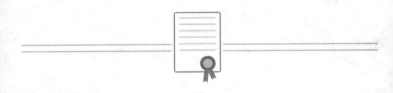

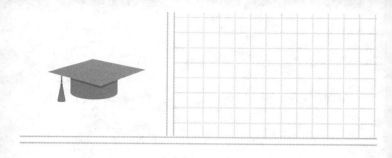

*And when I was burdened with worries,
you comforted me and made me feel secure.*

PSALM 94:19 CEV

Gratitude

*Always be joyful and never stop
praying. Whatever happens, keep
thanking God because of Jesus Christ.
This is what God wants you to do.*
1 THESSALONIANS 5:16–18 CEV

How can we be thankful for *everything*? Seems like a high call. It makes sense to be grateful for blessings, but for hardship and troubles as well? This is the Bible's call. Even in our darkest circumstances, we can find a reason to be grateful. Gratitude transforms our hearts from dark and moody and grumbling to bright and hopeful and alive. No matter what happens, look for a reason to praise God. It will transform your soul.

There is always something to be thankful for! Paul found it in prison. David found it on the run. No matter where life takes you or what your circumstances, there is something you can find to give thanks to God for. Ask the Lord to give you a thankful heart.

Do you ever forget to do important things? Sometimes we forget we want to exercise or eat right or even that we want to memorize scripture. Our minds are so filled with deadlines and passwords and facts and figures that the really important things can slip our minds. Technology can help us remember.

Here are some ways technology can be used to remind you of the things you don't want to forget:

▸ If you have a smart phone, make a copy of a verse you want to memorize as your wallpaper.

▸ Set an alarm on your phone or watch with a reminder to pause and say thanks to God for something.

▸ Write notes to yourself with verses you want to memorize and e-mail them to yourself.

▸ Set a calendar item as a "verse of the day."

*And whatever you do or say, do it as a
representative of the Lord Jesus, giving
thanks through him to God the Father.*
COLOSSIANS 3:17 NLT

*Praise the LORD. Give thanks to the LORD,
for he is good, his love endures forever.*
PSALM 106:1 NIV

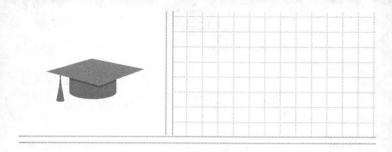

*Don't worry about anything; instead,
pray about everything. Tell God what you need,
and thank him for all he has done.*

<small>PHILIPPIANS 4:6 NLT</small>

Temptation

*God is faithful. He will not allow the
temptation to be more than you can stand.
When you are tempted, he will show you
a way out so that you can endure.*
1 Corinthians 10:13 NLT

This world carries many temptations: power, sex, money, greed. Each day we are given the choice to give in to temptations or overcome them. Some are obvious—we don't go near them. Others are much more insidious, sneaking their way into our lives before we know what hits us.

These verses in 1 Corinthians provide a consistent and sure model for living our lives above temptation. First, we must never think we are too strong to fall. Second, we must remember that we are not alone! Our vulnerability to temptation is shared by every human being from the beginning of time. Even Jesus was tempted and proved it is possible for a human to resist. Finally, we must trust our Father. When we focus on the Lord, we are reminded of His great promise: that He will never let us be tempted beyond what we can bear.

Trust Him today to overcome temptation.

If you have ever taken an English class or written an essay, you were no doubt told to use lots of action words in your writing. Without verbs, writing is bland and passive. With them, stories become alive. We are transported into the mind of the writer, practically feeling in our souls what that author wants to convey.

Scripture is filled with action words. These are not just letters on a page, but an active, alive handbook for our lives. The Holy Spirit resides within these verbs and makes them a part of our very souls.

Resisting temptation is an active process. As you commit the following verses to memory, copy down all the verbs and memorize them separately. You will be surprised how alive these words become. Can you imagine the devil running from you as you surrender your life to God?

*Surrender to God! Resist the devil,
and he will run from you.*
JAMES 4:7 CEV

*He personally carried our sins in his body on the
cross so that we can be dead to sin and live for
what is right. By his wounds you are healed.*
1 PETER 2:24 NLT

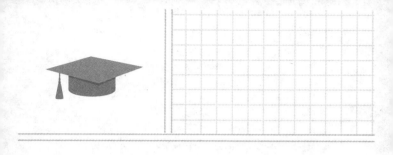

*You must stop doing anything immoral
or evil. Instead be humble and accept
the message that is planted in you to save you.*

JAMES 1:21 CEV

The Seed of Conflict

You want what you don't have, so you scheme and kill to get it. You are jealous of what others have, but you can't get it, so you fight and wage war to take it away from them. Yet you don't have what you want because you don't ask God for it.

JAMES 4:2 NLT

Conflict. It's an ugly word, and many of us try to avoid it. It is unlikely that we have ever thought of killing someone who didn't give us what we wanted. On the other hand, look at 1 John 3:15: "If you hate each other, you are murderers, and we know that murderers do not have eternal life" (CEV). The language is strong, the message clear. When we focus on what others have and what we lack, this breeds within us a hateful, murderous rage that is the source of much conflict. We question whether God really loves us. We start to resent our brothers or sisters. When we are jealous, this is a strong indication that we are not trusting God to meet our needs.

There are more than enough of God's rich blessings to go around. Keep your focus on Him, rather than others. Ask for what you need. Trust Him to provide.

When we experience an uncomfortable emotion like jealousy or anger or pride, we often have a tendency to deny it, to pretend we're not feeling it. Burying our emotions causes problems later and can be the source of a great deal of conflict. The Bible shares wisdom for avoiding conflict. One helpful strategy is to identify emotions before we express them. If someone makes us angry, we can step back and ask ourselves what it is we are feeling. We can first take the anger to God and ask Him what we should do with it.

Turn the words of 1 Corinthians 13:4–7 into a prayer. Bring your uncomfortable emotions to God and ask Him to transform them through the power of His love.

A gentle answer deflects anger,
but harsh words make tempers flare.
PROVERBS 15:1 NLT

Everyone should be quick to listen,
slow to speak and slow to become
angry, because human anger does not
produce the righteousness that God desires.
JAMES 1:19–20 NIV

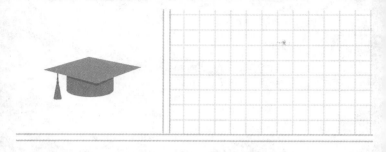

Love is kind and patient, never jealous, boastful, proud, or rude. Love isn't selfish or quick tempered. It doesn't keep a record of wrongs that others do. Love rejoices in the truth, but not in evil. Love is always supportive, loyal, hopeful, and trusting.

1 Corinthians 13:4–7 CEV

Loving God

Hear, O Israel: The LORD our God, the LORD is one. Love the LORD your God with all your heart and with all your soul and with all your strength.

DEUTERONOMY 6:4–5 NIV

In Acts 13:22, Luke tells us that God called David a man after his own heart. There is no doubt that David was a great man. Through the Psalms we learn a lot about his heart—how he longed for God's Word, how he cried out to Him for mercy, how thankful he was for God's blessings. David wasn't perfect—far from it. He committed adultery and murder. He lied. In Psalm 51, David pours out his heart to God, grieving over his sin with Bathsheba.

Loving God doesn't mean we will always be perfect. It does mean that we continue to seek Him; that we take Him all of our emotions, thoughts, worries, and cares; and that we admit when we've done wrong and ask for His forgiveness. Loving God is far less about perfection and much more about surrender. How can you surrender your heart to God today?

A truly loving relationship spans the depths of human emotion. Through ups and downs and joys and sorrows, love remains faithful, steadfast, and true. The Psalms give us unique insight into a heart that is madly in love with God.

Sometimes it is worshipful:

Because of your great mercy, I come to your house, LORD, and I am filled with wonder as I bow down to worship at your holy temple.
PSALM 5:7 CEV

Other times it is thankful:

I will praise the LORD God with a song and a thankful heart.
PSALM 69:30 CEV

It is sometimes desperate:

Have mercy on me, LORD, for I am faint; heal me, LORD, for my bones are in agony.
PSALM 6:2 NIV

But through it all, it continually looks to God, in reverent awe:

The whole earth is filled with awe at your wonders; where morning dawns, where evening fades, you call forth songs of joy.
PSALM 65:8 NIV

As you prepare to memorize these verses, read them carefully, out loud if possible. What heart qualities does each describe?

My heart has heard you say, "Come and talk with me." And my heart responds, "LORD, I am coming."
PSALM 27:8 NLT

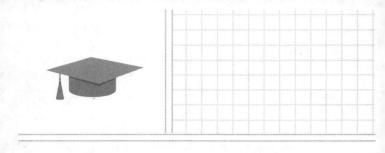

"*Those who accept my commandments
and obey them are the ones who love me.
And because they love me, my Father
will love them. And I will love them
and reveal myself to each of them.*"

JOHN 14:21 NLT

The Freedom of Truth

Jesus said to the people who believed in him, "You are truly my disciples if you remain faithful to my teachings. And you will know the truth, and the truth will set you free."

JOHN 8:31–32 NLT

Jesus confused His listeners. By saying they would be "set free" He implied they were slaves. They were quick to correct Him in the next verse. "We are the children of Abraham!" they cried. Their pride was evident. "We've never been slaves to anyone!"

Of course, Jesus uses this metaphor to explain our relationship to sin. We are either in bondage or we are His children. If we are His children, we are members of His family and have all the rights and privileges that come with being His children. Sin enslaves us, but truth frees us. The truth of who Jesus is and what He has done gives us freedom to live as His children, free and unfettered by the shackles of sin.

The wise man built his house upon the rock,
The wise man built his house upon the rock,
The wise man built his house upon the rock,
. . . the house on the rock stood firm.

The children's song, in its simplicity, reminds us to build our lives on the truth of God's Word. In Matthew 7:24, Jesus says, "Anyone who listens to my teaching and follows it is wise, like a person who builds a house on solid rock" (NLT). Building our lives on this truth means that we can stand firm through all of life's storms and prepare to spend an eternity with Him in our heavenly home.

Memorizing His Word strengthens that foundation in both your heart and your mind. To remind yourself of the Word memorization you have done, consider creating a scrapbook with all the verses you have committed to memory. Find pictures to illustrate each one or write a short story telling how the verse has impacted your life. Throughout your life you will find yourself turning to it again and again. Rejoice in this firm foundation!

*Let your roots grow down into him,
and let your lives be built on him. Then your faith
will grow strong in the truth you were taught,
and you will overflow with thankfulness.*

COLOSSIANS 2:7 NLT

*Therefore each of you must put off falsehood
and speak truthfully to your neighbor,
for we are all members of one body.*

EPHESIANS 4:25 NIV

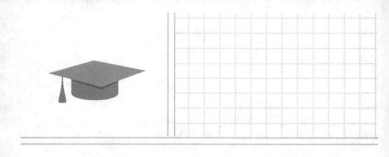

*Make them holy by your truth; teach
them your word, which is truth.*

JOHN 17:17 NLT

Scripture Index

About the Author

Joanna Bloss is a personal trainer, writer, and student living in the midwest. She's a coauthor of *Grit for the Oyster: 250 Pearls of Wisdom for Aspiring Authors.*